NOV___
THE HOLY SPIRIT
with St. Alphonsus

Adapted by David Werthmann

Liguori

Imprimi Potest: Stephen T. Rehrauer, CSsR, Provincial
Denver Province, the Redemptorists

ISBN 978-0-7648-2845-4

Published by Liguori Publications, Liguori, Missouri 63057

Copyright © 2021 Liguori Publications

To order, visit Liguori.org or call 800-325-9521.

Liguori Publications, a nonprofit corporation, is an apostolate of the Redemptorists. To learn more about the Redemptorists, visit Redemptorists.com.

Printed in the United States of America

25 24 23 22 21 / 5 4 3 2 1

First Edition

Cover detail: © "Saint Alphonsus Liguori" by Joan Cole, Courtesy of Trinity Stores, www.trinitystores.com, 800.699.4482.

The Patron of Confessors

Saint Alphonsus Liguori (1696–1787) was born into a family of Italian nobility. He earned law degrees in civil and canon law by age sixteen. Upon recognizing corruption within the legal system, he became a priest and founded the Congregation of the Most Holy Redeemer, commonly known as the Redemptorists, in 1732. The mission of his priests and brothers is to serve people who are "poor and most abandoned." In 1762, he was appointed a bishop. He was ninety when he died in 1787. Pope Gregory XVI canonized him in 1839, and Pope Pius IX named him a doctor of the Church in 1871. Saint Alphonsus' feast day is August 1.

Alphonsus, who wrote extensively on issues of spirituality and morality, is the patron of confessors. This novena is adapted from one of the many devotionals he wrote for Redemptorist priests and brothers, but it is relevant for everyone. In this shortened version, some of the images have been updated to make them easier to understand for modern readers.

What Is a *Novena*?

Traditionally, a *novena* is a prayer or set of prayers repeated for nine consecutive days. However, it could just as well be accomplished in nine consecutive hours of one day or be spread out to include one particular day each week over nine weeks. For example, those who participate in the Eucharist on the first Friday of each month make a novena of first Fridays.

No fixed rules are required for making a novena, except to persevere in the prayer. So a novena is a good way to help us form the habit of regular prayer.

Novenas can help us focus on a particular aspect or image of God amid our daily life. Our devotion helps us live steeped in deep love for God and neighbor. Through these prayers and devotions, we invite God into our hearts and share with him our needs and worries. We ask God to accept our prayers and, as we do, our relationship with the Divine One grows.

The Holy Spirit

Among all Christian doctrines, the Trinity is perhaps the most difficult to comprehend. It declares that God is a single being yet three distinct persons. We also believe that God is eternal and existed before the creation of the universe. Saint John defines God simply as "love" (see 1 John 4:8, 16). As we know, love must be shared and expressed or it doesn't exist. So if "God love" existed before creation, it had to have someone to love or it could not have existed. Thus, the Christian tradition maintains that, as love, God exists in a single living being and within the dynamic of perfect, intimate love flowing among the three persons who comprise the one being we call Father, Son, and Holy Spirit. This is a mystery that is beyond our limited human comprehension, and we will go crazy if we try to figure it out! Yet it is what we profess.

After Jesus appeared to his disciples several times to witness that he truly had risen from the dead, he then prepared to ascend into heaven, and he promised that his Spirit would remain with us here on earth at all times: "And I will ask the Father, and he will give you another Advocate to be with you always" (John 14:16). That "Advocate" is the Holy Spirit whom Jesus sent to be the presence of God always among us. The Holy Spirit constantly nudges us along to do the right thing in our lives.

I hope this booklet can help deepen your awareness of the Holy Spirit's impact in your life and in our world. Most of all, may it help you grow in your love for God.

DAVID WERTHMANN

HOW TO USE THIS BOOKLET

When making this novena privately, try to find a place where you can be comfortable and quiet, away from distractions. Begin by closing your eyes and becoming aware of the Holy Spirit's presence with you in that place, at that moment. Before beginning the prayers that follow, call to mind what you want to ask of the Holy Spirit.

Opening Prayer

O Holy Spirit, I believe that you are eternally one with the Father and the Son. I now ask you to help me to grow in holiness by entering my heart to enlighten it and soften it. You overshadowed the Virgin Mary when she conceived. Then, on the first Pentecost you gave the apostles courage and zeal to carry out our Lord's mission throughout the whole world. Now I pray: Come Holy Spirit, fill the hearts of your faithful ones and enkindle in us the fire of your love. Amen.

Litany to the Holy Spirit

Spirit of God, who inflames our hearts,
    hear my prayer.

Spirit of God, who enlightens our souls,
    hear my prayer.

Spirit of God, fountain of all graces,
    hear my prayer.

Spirit of love, who remains with us always,
    hear my prayer.

Spirit of love, who calms our restlessness,
    hear my prayer.

Spirit of love, who binds us to the Father
    and the Son,
    hear my prayer.

Spirit of strength, who helps us grow in virtue,
    hear my prayer.

Spirit of presence, through whom God dwells
    in our hearts,
    hear my prayer.

Treasure of love, who contains all goodness,
    hear my prayer.

***Now proceed to one of the nine meditations
on the following pages.***

MEDITATION 1

Love Is a Fire that Inflames the Heart

My heart smolders within me.
In my sighing a fire blazes up.

PSALM 39:4

In Jewish law, God said a fire should burn continuously on his altar (see Leviticus 6:2, 5). Jesus declared, "I have come to set the earth on fire, and how I wish it were already blazing!" (Luke 12:49). He meant that he wants everyone's heart to be on fire with a passionate love for God and neighbor. So today we can consider our own hearts as the altars where God desires that the fire of divine love should always burn. Once ascended to heaven, Jesus sent the Holy Spirit who appeared as tongues of fire (see Acts of the Apostles 2:3). Thus, God gives us the Holy Spirit to dwell in our hearts and keep them constantly on fire with love.

That same Spirit is the holy fire that inspired saints to do great things for God—to love their enemies and sometimes embrace death for the sake of God's kingdom. Love never says, "That's enough." People who love God want to do even more to show God their love any way they can. The "fire" of the Holy Spirit is fueled by prayer. Thus, if we wish to burn with love for God, we must love to pray, because prayer is what ignites a deep love for God.

Imagine someone in your life who loves you very much, perhaps your mother, your spouse, or an exceptionally close friend. (Pause) Multiply that person's love by 10,000 times to estimate how much God loves you! Sit quietly for a few moments and soak in all the love God has for you.

PRAYER

Spirit of God, inflame in me a desire to carry on your work. While living on earth, Jesus frequently called upon the Father. Like him, I will call on you often to ask for your help in sharing your goodness and your infinite love with all whom I encounter. Mary, my mother, set my heart on fire with as much love for God as you have. Amen.

MEDITATION 2

Love Is a Light that Enlightens the Soul

For you, LORD, give light to my lamp;
my God brightens my darkness.

PSALM 18:29

The Holy Spirit not only inflames our hearts so we can love God even more, it also dispels our darkness. For example, the Spirit makes us aware of God's goodness and the tremendous love God deserves because of the boundless love he shows us. The Spirit also shows us the vanity of earthly goods versus the great value of eternal things. People who are absorbed in earthly pleasures do not appreciate this. Rather, they remain attached to what they ought to avoid and neglect those they should love.

Perhaps God seems to be loved by so few people because many of them hardly know who God really is. If we don't *know* God, then how can we *love* God? Saints, both known and unknown, constantly seek enlightenment from the Holy Spirit to know our loving God more fully. Without the Holy Spirit guiding us, we cannot find God, and we cannot avoid stumbling into sin.

What concept comes to mind when you think of God? (Pause) Is your notion of God easy to love? Do you find yourself wanting to spend time with God as you might enjoy being with a favorite grandparent or a best friend? Do you believe that God, as you imagine him to be, truly hears your prayers?

································ **PRAYER** ································

O Holy Spirit, I realize that you are the giver of all light. Even though I have often refused to open my eyes to your light, you have never stopped shining it on me. Please let your light draw me into your love. Help me appreciate your infinite goodness more and more. Give me strength to love you with my whole heart along with each of my family members and neighbors. Mother Mary, intercede for me always. Amen.

MEDITATION 3

Love Is a Fountain that Satisfies

For with you is the fountain of life.

PSALM 36:10

In Jesus' well-known encounter with the Samaritan woman at the well he tells her, "whoever drinks the water I shall give will never thirst" (John 4:14). God's love satisfies all thirsts. The person who truly loves God does not look anywhere else because in God we find everything we need.

Many people go around seeking earthly pleasures that do not last. Yet God, who loves us so much and desires our love in return, pleads with us: "Let anyone who thirsts come to me and drink" (John 7:37). God will never turn anyone away. Thus, those who want to be truly happy should seek out Jesus who will give them the Holy Spirit. At the well, Jesus continued by quoting Scripture: "Whoever believes in me, as scripture says: 'Rivers of living water will flow from within him'" (John 7:38). Christ promises that those who love him will receive a multitude of life-giving riches flowing from the Holy Spirit, both for themselves and for others.

The key that opens the channel of these flowing riches is prayer. Prayer obtains everything good for us, for as Jesus promised, "Ask and you will receive" (John 16:24). We humans are spiritually blind, poor, and weak. But through prayer we receive light, strength, and an abundance of grace. We simply have to ask for those things in prayer.

What do you thirst for most in your life? (Pause) Are you seeking to satisfy that "thirst" in the right places?

PRAYER

O Jesus, like the Samaritan woman I ask you to give me this water of your love. You have already showered me with so many good things. May your Spirit fill my soul with grace so it may bring forth fruits for God's reign here on earth. O Holy Spirit, fountain of living water, help my loved ones and me remain faithful to you. Mary, my hope, keep me always under your protection. Amen.

MEDITATION 4

Love Is Like the Nourishing Morning Dew

The land will yield its crops,
and the heavens will yield their dew.

ZECHARIAH 8:12

We seldom realize how important morning dew is for nourishing the grass of our lawn. Similarly, God's love nourishes our virtuous desires and good works. Those are the fruits that the grace of the Holy Spirit produces. God's love also cools the temptations that lie deep in our hearts. Such "dew" descends into our hearts during prayer. Fifteen minutes spent with God in prayer may be enough to subdue most feelings of hatred when they arise, or any passions toward sinfulness we might be holding onto.

Saint Paul points out that "the Spirit too comes to the aid of our weakness; for we do not know how to pray as we ought" (Romans 8:26). Quiet meditation practiced frequently is the foundation upon which love remains firm so that we are prompted to love our neighbor as ourselves, and to love God above everything else (see Luke 10:27). During periods of meditation we try to set aside earthly cares in order to give God's Spirit an opportunity to speak to our hearts. Anyone who truly loves God prays regularly. Without prayer it is impossible to grow in holiness.

Recall how you first learned to pray as a child. (Pause) Compare that to how you pray now. (Pause) Then reflect on how the Holy Spirit has led your prayer life to develop and deepen through the years as your relationship with God has changed and matured.

PRAYER

O Holy Spirit, help me in my prayer. Enter my heart and teach me to pray as I need to. Strengthen me to pray even in times of weariness or spiritual dryness. Give me such a desire to pray that I may regularly converse with you in prayer throughout my day. I want to grow in holiness so that I may love you more. O God, I will spend my days loving you by loving and serving my family members and my neighbors in need. O Mary, my hope, protect me. Amen.

MEDITATION 5

Love Provides Rest that Refreshes the Soul

[Jesus said,] "Come to me, all you who labor and are burdened, and I will give you rest."

MATTHEW 11:28

When people are in love, they forget all the cares of the world when they are together. Love unites their hearts despite differences they may have, and life is just not the same when they are apart. Similarly, divine love unites we who are loved to God who loves us. If we deeply love God, we can be confident of the Holy Spirit's constant presence and care for us.

Unfortunately, pains and tribulations occur in everyone's life. Yet when we are confronted with some sort of "cross" in life, the Holy Spirit reminds us that we never carry it alone. That's because we are helped by Jesus Christ who carries all our crosses along with us. That belief should comfort anyone seeking to deepen his or her relationship with God. It means we can trust the Spirit's guidance to help us get through any loss, any trial, or any suffering that afflicts us. Then we will find peace and contentment—even encouragement in the knowledge that God's love for us is endless. And that brings "the peace of God, that surpasses all understanding" (Philippians 4:7).

Think about how you felt when you experienced unconditional love from a parent, spouse, or a dear friend who helped you get through a particularly difficult time. (Pause) Are you able to express that kind of love—that is, God's love—toward others?

PRAYER

While I often profess my love for you, O God, I frequently find myself forgetting that you are always with me. I regret how often I have not trusted in your love and support. Holy Spirit, help me become more and more aware of your presence in my life so I may follow your guidance and grow in holiness. Show me the right path for my life. Lord, I truly want my love for you to grow. Mary, my mother, I trust in you to help me, as well! Amen.

MEDITATION 6

Love Is the Virtue that Gives Us Strength

Love is strong as Death.

SONG OF SONGS 8:6

Young people often feel invincible. Old age and infirmity seem to be in the far distant future for them. While no one can avoid sickness or eventual death, love can overcome any great difficulty. Love conquers all—all sorrows, all losses, even death itself. Whenever we are asked to do something for someone we love, we never hesitate. Whether the task requires a little inconvenience or great sacrifice on our part, we carry it out nevertheless because of our love for that person. Saint Augustine suggested that when we love someone, we experience one of two possible feelings: either doing even difficult things for someone we love is not hard at all; or although a task may be difficult, we love doing it simply because we love the person for whom we're doing it.

God's love for us is completely unconditional. It never changes. Our love for God should be the same. Even the martyrs continued to feel the presence of

God's love sheltering them and were strengthened to bear their torments. We can be sure that we truly love the Divine One when we are as faithful to God in difficult times as we are in prosperous times.

It is one thing to pray for things we need or want—and God already knows about those—but how easy is it for you to pray when things are not going well for you? (Pause) When you simply do not know which way to turn in life? When it feels like God is not listening?

PRAYER

O God, you are all goodness and love. Come fill my heart and live there so I may always belong to you. I love you, Lord, so I have confidence that you already live in my heart. Therefore, increase my love for you so I may also love others more, especially my family members and my neighbors in need. Mary, help me persevere in loving your Son, as well as my sisters and brothers on earth. Amen.

MEDITATION 7

Love Allows God to Live in Our Hearts

God is love, and whoever remains in love remains in God, and God in him.

1 JOHN 4:16

Jesus promised us, "If you love me, you will keep my commandments. And I will ask the Father, and he will give you another Advocate to be with you always, the Spirit of truth" (John 14:15–17). The Holy Spirit surrounds us at all times like the air we breathe. It is constantly nudging us along to do the right thing.

God's Spirit dwells in every human soul. Yet that is not enough because God desires in return that we love him as much as we possibly can. We can never doubt that our Lord deserves our love. After all, Jesus gave his blood and his life for us on the cross, and today he continues to give us his Body and Blood in the Eucharist. There is nothing more he can give. So how could we ever limit the love we owe him in return? How could we possibly allow the love we owe God to be divided among all the distractions that this world puts before us: fame, wealth, popularity, power? Such things can squeeze God out of our lives, and we must guard against that happening.

Pause to ask yourself these questions: How often do I pray each day—even if only for a few moments? Do I regularly attend Mass and receive holy Communion? Do I give my full loving attention to someone who is in distress or asking for help? What other ways may God be asking me to open my heart and let in his love?

PRAYER

O God, I realize that you desire that I love you above all things and to love my neighbor as myself. I have often ignored your presence within me, and yet you never leave me alone. I now ask for the grace to never again forget that you are with me always. You seek me, and so I promise to seek you more and more every day by recognizing your presence in all creation, especially in my fellow human beings. Mother Mary, I trust in your help to grow in love for your Son and for my neighbor. Amen.

MEDITATION 8

Love Binds Us to God

Whoever does not love does not know God,
for God is love.

1 JOHN 4:8

In his first epistle, quoted above, St. John defines God simply as love—nothing more. The entire universe was created, or sprang forth, from the superabundant love that the Father, Son, and Holy Spirit share with each other. Just as the power of love is what binds the Trinity together, likewise love also binds us to God. Among the greatest ways God expresses love for us and draws us to himself are: the sacrifice Jesus made on the cross; God's constant presence among us in the Eucharist; and the gift of the Holy Spirit.

How can we show our love in return? Scripture tells us: "Whoever does not love a brother whom he has seen cannot love God whom he has not seen" (1 John 4:20). It also points out that love, or charity, is the greatest of all virtues (see 1 Corinthians 13:13). Thus, the best way we can strive to strengthen our ties of love for God are through acts of charity and love toward our neighbors who are most in need.

Take a moment to think about someone who is elderly or poor, sick or alone, or helpless in some way. What can you do for that person to help ease his or her struggles? As individuals, none of us can end poverty and sickness in the world, but at least we can make one person's life better in some simple way each day.

PRAYER

Dear God, you have done so much to show your love for us. I admit that at times I neglect to respond to your love in appropriate ways. Holy Spirit, inspire me to know how I can best express my love for you. Give me strength every day to love you by loving the people you have placed in my life, both at home and at work. Queen of Heaven, guide me to know how I can best love your Son, especially through those whom I encounter each day. Amen.

MEDITATION 9

Love Is a Treasure that Contains All Goodness

For she is an unfailing treasure; / those who gain this treasure win the friendship of God.

WISDOM 7:14

It is natural for humans to seek things that will bring us happiness. However, if we seek these only among what we find here on earth, we will never obtain total contentment. But if we seek God, our yearnings will be fully satisfied because everything that is good comes from God.

The psalmist encourages us: "Find your delight in the LORD / who will give you your heart's desire" (Psalm 37:4). Think about St. John Paul II or St. Teresa of Calcutta. Weren't they among the most joyful people in the world? It is because they sought after and found God. Each of them developed a deep relationship with God through regular prayer and constant concern for others. Bring to mind friends or acquaintances who always seem to spread happiness and joy wherever they go. What do you suppose is their secret?

If we recognize the great treasure of divine love and seek to grow in it, we will be truly blessed because nothing else in life will matter as much as God's love. What are some earthly treasures and desires that keep you from loving God and neighbor as God calls us to? (Pause)

--- **PRAYER** ---

Lord, I am comforted by the words of Scripture: "The LORD is good to those who trust in him,/ to the one that seeks him" (Lamentations 3:25). That belief confirms for me that when we seek you, we find a treasure of total goodness. Make my heart happy by filling it with your love. O Holy Spirit, may your "holy fire" purify anything within me that does not help me to love you as I wish. Mary, my mother, help me by your prayers, too! Amen.

Gifts of the Holy Spirit

Wisdom
to enlighten our minds and draw us to God

Understanding
to recognize truth and realize our purpose in life

Counsel
to judge rightly with prudence

Fortitude
to stand up for what is right with courage and endurance

Knowledge
to see all things and persons with love, as God sees them

Piety
to rely totally on God with reverence and humility

Wonder and awe
to joyfully recognize God's glory and grandeur

Additional Prayers to the Holy Spirit

(Glory Be) Doxology

Glory be to the Father, and to the Son, and to the Holy Spirit; as it was in the beginning, is now, and ever shall be, world without end. Amen.

St. Augustine's Prayer to the Holy Spirit

Breathe in me, O Holy Spirit, that my thoughts may all be holy. Act in me, O Holy Spirit, that my work, too, may be holy. Draw my heart, O Holy Spirit, that I love but what is holy. Strengthen me, O Holy Spirit, to defend all that is holy. Guard me, then, O Holy Spirit, that I always may be holy. Amen.

Come, Holy Spirit, Creator Blest
Veni Creator Spiritus

Come, Holy Spirit, Creator blest,
and in our souls take up Thy rest;
come with Thy grace and heavenly aid
to fill the hearts which Thou hast made.

O comforter, to Thee we cry,
O heavenly gift of God Most High,
O fount of life and fire of love,
and sweet anointing from above.

Thou in Thy sevenfold gifts are known;
Thou, finger of God's hand we own;
Thou, promise of the Father, Thou
Who dost the tongue with power imbue.

Kindle our sense from above,
and make our hearts o'erflow with love;
with patience firm and virtue high
the weakness of our flesh supply.

Far from us drive the foe we dread,
and grant us Thy peace instead;
so shall we not, with Thee for guide,
turn from the path of life aside.

Oh, may Thy grace on us bestow
the Father and the Son to know;
and Thee, through endless times confessed,
of both the eternal Spirit blest.

Now to the Father and the Son,
Who rose from death, be glory given,
with Thou, O Holy Comforter,
henceforth by all in earth and heaven. Amen.

David Werthmann has a master's degree in pastoral studies with an emphasis on spirituality from the Aquinas Institute of Theology in St. Louis. He did further graduate studies in pastoral liturgy at Santa Clara University in California. For more than thirty years, David has been a teacher, a pastoral minister, a liturgical musician, and a freelance writer. He is active as a eucharistic minister in his local parish in St. Louis and serves on the parish antiracism team.